This Stone & Minerals
Geology Journal Belongs To

_____

If Found Please Contact

_____

Finding Index

01 _____

02 _____

03 _____

04 _____

05 _____

06 _____

07 _____

08 _____

09 _____

10 _____

11 _____

12 _____

13 _____

14 _____

15 _____

16 _____

17 _____

18 _____

19 _____

20 _____

21 _____

22 _____

23 _____

24 _____

25 _____

26 _____

27 _____

28 _____

29 _____

30 _____

31 _____

32 _____

33 _____

34 _____

35 _____

36 _____

37 _____

38 _____

39 _____

40 _____

41 _____

42 _____

43 _____

44 _____

45 _____

46 _____

47 _____

48 _____

49 _____

50 _____

51 _____

52 _____

53 _____

54 _____

55 _____

56 _____

57 _____

58 _____

59 _____

60 _____

61 _____

62 _____

63 _____

64 _____

65 _____

66 _____

67 _____

68 _____

69 _____

70 _____

71 _____

72 _____

73 _____

74 _____

75 _____

76 _____

77 _____

78 _____

79 _____

80 _____

81 _____

82 _____

83 _____

84 _____

85 _____

86 _____

87 _____

88 _____

89 _____

90 _____

91 _____

92 _____

93 _____

94 _____

95 _____

96 _____

97 _____

98 _____

99 _____

100 _____

DATE

TIME

LOCATION

ENVIRONMENT

☐ FOREST	☐ GRASSLAND
☐ DESERT	☐ TUNDRA
☐ FRESHWATER	☐ MARINE

TYPE

SHAPE

WEIGHT

COLORS

TEXTURE

LUSTER

SKETCH / SAMPLE

LENGTH	WIDTH	DEPTH

EQUIPMENT

-
-
-

SETTINGS

EXTENDED DESCRIPTION

DATE

TIME

LOCATION

ENVIRONMENT

☐ FOREST	☐ GRASSLAND
☐ DESERT	☐ TUNDRA
☐ FRESHWATER	☐ MARINE

TYPE

SHAPE

WEIGHT

COLORS

TEXTURE

LUSTER

SKETCH / SAMPLE

LENGTH	WIDTH	DEPTH

EQUIPMENT

-
-
-

SETTINGS

EXTENDED DESCRIPTION

📅 DATE	
🕐 TIME	
📍 LOCATION	

ENVIRONMENT

☐ FOREST	☐ GRASSLAND
☐ DESERT	☐ TUNDRA
☐ FRESHWATER	☐ MARINE

◇ TYPE	
▽ SHAPE	
⚖ WEIGHT	

⊛ COLORS
▨ TEXTURE
✦ LUSTER

SKETCH / SAMPLE

LENGTH	WIDTH	DEPTH

EQUIPMENT

•
•
•
⚏ SETTINGS

EXTENDED DESCRIPTION

DATE

TIME

LOCATION

ENVIRONMENT

☐ FOREST	☐ GRASSLAND
☐ DESERT	☐ TUNDRA
☐ FRESHWATER	☐ MARINE

TYPE

SHAPE

WEIGHT

COLORS

TEXTURE

LUSTER

SKETCH / SAMPLE

LENGTH	WIDTH	DEPTH

EQUIPMENT

-
-
-

SETTINGS

EXTENDED DESCRIPTION

DATE

TIME

LOCATION

ENVIRONMENT

☐ FOREST	☐ GRASSLAND
☐ DESERT	☐ TUNDRA
☐ FRESHWATER	☐ MARINE

TYPE

SHAPE

WEIGHT

COLORS

TEXTURE

LUSTER

SKETCH / SAMPLE

LENGTH	WIDTH	DEPTH

EQUIPMENT

-
-
-

SETTINGS

EXTENDED DESCRIPTION

📅 DATE	SKETCH / SAMPLE
🕐 TIME	
📍 LOCATION	

ENVIRONMENT

☐ FOREST	☐ GRASSLAND
☐ DESERT	☐ TUNDRA
☐ FRESHWATER	☐ MARINE

🔷 TYPE

🔻 SHAPE

⚖️ WEIGHT

LENGTH	WIDTH	DEPTH

🔵 COLORS

▨ TEXTURE

✦ LUSTER

EQUIPMENT

·

·

·

⚙ SETTINGS

EXTENDED DESCRIPTION

DATE

TIME

LOCATION

ENVIRONMENT

☐ FOREST	☐ GRASSLAND
☐ DESERT	☐ TUNDRA
☐ FRESHWATER	☐ MARINE

TYPE

SHAPE

WEIGHT

COLORS

TEXTURE

LUSTER

SKETCH / SAMPLE

LENGTH	WIDTH	DEPTH

EQUIPMENT

- .
- .
- .

SETTINGS

EXTENDED DESCRIPTION

📅 DATE	SKETCH / SAMPLE
🕙 TIME	
📍 LOCATION	

ENVIRONMENT

☐ FOREST	☐ GRASSLAND
☐ DESERT	☐ TUNDRA
☐ FRESHWATER	☐ MARINE

🔺 TYPE
🔻 SHAPE
⚖️ WEIGHT

LENGTH	WIDTH	DEPTH

⊛ COLORS
▨ TEXTURE
✦ LUSTER

EQUIPMENT

-
-
-

⚊ SETTINGS

EXTENDED DESCRIPTION

DATE

TIME

LOCATION

ENVIRONMENT

☐ FOREST	☐ GRASSLAND
☐ DESERT	☐ TUNDRA
☐ FRESHWATER	☐ MARINE

TYPE

SHAPE

WEIGHT

COLORS

TEXTURE

LUSTER

SKETCH / SAMPLE

LENGTH	WIDTH	DEPTH

EQUIPMENT

-
-
-

SETTINGS

EXTENDED DESCRIPTION

DATE

TIME

LOCATION

ENVIRONMENT

☐ FOREST	☐ GRASSLAND
☐ DESERT	☐ TUNDRA
☐ FRESHWATER	☐ MARINE

TYPE

SHAPE

WEIGHT

COLORS

TEXTURE

LUSTER

SKETCH / SAMPLE

LENGTH	WIDTH	DEPTH

EQUIPMENT

- .
- .
- .

SETTINGS

EXTENDED DESCRIPTION

DATE

TIME

LOCATION

ENVIRONMENT

☐ FOREST	☐ GRASSLAND
☐ DESERT	☐ TUNDRA
☐ FRESHWATER	☐ MARINE

TYPE

SHAPE

WEIGHT

COLORS

TEXTURE

LUSTER

SKETCH / SAMPLE

LENGTH	WIDTH	DEPTH

EQUIPMENT

-
-
-

SETTINGS

EXTENDED DESCRIPTION

DATE

TIME

LOCATION

ENVIRONMENT

☐ FOREST	☐ GRASSLAND
☐ DESERT	☐ TUNDRA
☐ FRESHWATER	☐ MARINE

TYPE

SHAPE

WEIGHT

COLORS

TEXTURE

LUSTER

SKETCH / SAMPLE

LENGTH	WIDTH	DEPTH

EQUIPMENT

-
-
-

SETTINGS

EXTENDED DESCRIPTION

DATE

TIME

LOCATION

ENVIRONMENT

☐ FOREST	☐ GRASSLAND
☐ DESERT	☐ TUNDRA
☐ FRESHWATER	☐ MARINE

TYPE

SHAPE

WEIGHT

COLORS

TEXTURE

LUSTER

SKETCH / SAMPLE

LENGTH	WIDTH	DEPTH

EQUIPMENT

-
-
-

SETTINGS

EXTENDED DESCRIPTION

DATE

TIME

LOCATION

ENVIRONMENT

☐ FOREST	☐ GRASSLAND
☐ DESERT	☐ TUNDRA
☐ FRESHWATER	☐ MARINE

TYPE

SHAPE

WEIGHT

COLORS

TEXTURE

LUSTER

SKETCH / SAMPLE

LENGTH	WIDTH	DEPTH

EQUIPMENT

-
-
-

SETTINGS

EXTENDED DESCRIPTION

DATE	**SKETCH / SAMPLE**
TIME	
LOCATION	

ENVIRONMENT

☐ FOREST	☐ GRASSLAND
☐ DESERT	☐ TUNDRA
☐ FRESHWATER	☐ MARINE

| **TYPE** |
| **SHAPE** |
| **WEIGHT** |

LENGTH	WIDTH	DEPTH

| **COLORS** |
| |
| **TEXTURE** |
| |
| **LUSTER** |
| |

EQUIPMENT

-
-
-

⚙ SETTINGS

EXTENDED DESCRIPTION

DATE

TIME

LOCATION

ENVIRONMENT

☐ FOREST	☐ GRASSLAND
☐ DESERT	☐ TUNDRA
☐ FRESHWATER	☐ MARINE

TYPE

SHAPE

WEIGHT

COLORS

TEXTURE

LUSTER

SKETCH / SAMPLE

LENGTH	WIDTH	DEPTH

EQUIPMENT

-
-
-

SETTINGS

EXTENDED DESCRIPTION

DATE

TIME

LOCATION

ENVIRONMENT

☐ FOREST	☐ GRASSLAND
☐ DESERT	☐ TUNDRA
☐ FRESHWATER	☐ MARINE

TYPE

SHAPE

WEIGHT

COLORS

TEXTURE

LUSTER

SKETCH / SAMPLE

LENGTH	WIDTH	DEPTH

EQUIPMENT

-
-
-

SETTINGS

EXTENDED DESCRIPTION

DATE

TIME

LOCATION

ENVIRONMENT

☐ FOREST	☐ GRASSLAND
☐ DESERT	☐ TUNDRA
☐ FRESHWATER	☐ MARINE

TYPE

SHAPE

WEIGHT

COLORS

TEXTURE

LUSTER

SKETCH / SAMPLE

LENGTH	WIDTH	DEPTH

EQUIPMENT

- .
- .
- .

SETTINGS

EXTENDED DESCRIPTION

DATE

TIME

LOCATION

ENVIRONMENT

☐ FOREST	☐ GRASSLAND
☐ DESERT	☐ TUNDRA
☐ FRESHWATER	☐ MARINE

TYPE

SHAPE

WEIGHT

COLORS

TEXTURE

LUSTER

SKETCH / SAMPLE

LENGTH	WIDTH	DEPTH

EQUIPMENT

-
-
-

⚙ SETTINGS

EXTENDED DESCRIPTION

DATE

TIME

LOCATION

ENVIRONMENT

- [ ] FOREST
- [ ] GRASSLAND
- [ ] DESERT
- [ ] TUNDRA
- [ ] FRESHWATER
- [ ] MARINE

TYPE

SHAPE

WEIGHT

COLORS

TEXTURE

LUSTER

SKETCH / SAMPLE

LENGTH	WIDTH	DEPTH

EQUIPMENT

- .
- .
- .

SETTINGS

EXTENDED DESCRIPTION

DATE	SKETCH / SAMPLE
TIME	
LOCATION	

ENVIRONMENT

☐ FOREST	☐ GRASSLAND
☐ DESERT	☐ TUNDRA
☐ FRESHWATER	☐ MARINE

TYPE
SHAPE
WEIGHT

LENGTH	WIDTH	DEPTH

COLORS

TEXTURE

LUSTER

EQUIPMENT

- .
- .
- .

SETTINGS

EXTENDED DESCRIPTION

DATE

TIME

LOCATION

ENVIRONMENT

☐ FOREST	☐ GRASSLAND
☐ DESERT	☐ TUNDRA
☐ FRESHWATER	☐ MARINE

TYPE

SHAPE

WEIGHT

COLORS

TEXTURE

LUSTER

SKETCH / SAMPLE

LENGTH	WIDTH	DEPTH

EQUIPMENT

-
-
-

SETTINGS

EXTENDED DESCRIPTION

DATE

TIME

LOCATION

ENVIRONMENT

☐ FOREST	☐ GRASSLAND
☐ DESERT	☐ TUNDRA
☐ FRESHWATER	☐ MARINE

TYPE

SHAPE

WEIGHT

COLORS

TEXTURE

LUSTER

SKETCH / SAMPLE

LENGTH	WIDTH	DEPTH

EQUIPMENT

-
-
-

SETTINGS

EXTENDED DESCRIPTION

📅 **DATE**		
🕐 **TIME**		
📍 **LOCATION**		

SKETCH / SAMPLE

ENVIRONMENT

☐ FOREST	☐ GRASSLAND
☐ DESERT	☐ TUNDRA
☐ FRESHWATER	☐ MARINE

🔺 **TYPE**		
🔻 **SHAPE**		
⚖️ **WEIGHT**		

LENGTH	WIDTH	DEPTH

⚛️ **COLORS**
🗂 **TEXTURE**
✨ **LUSTER**

EQUIPMENT

- .
- .
- .

🎚 SETTINGS

EXTENDED DESCRIPTION

DATE

TIME

LOCATION

ENVIRONMENT

☐	FOREST	☐	GRASSLAND
☐	DESERT	☐	TUNDRA
☐	FRESHWATER	☐	MARINE

TYPE

SHAPE

WEIGHT

COLORS

TEXTURE

LUSTER

SKETCH / SAMPLE

LENGTH	WIDTH	DEPTH

EQUIPMENT

- .
- .
- .

SETTINGS

EXTENDED DESCRIPTION

DATE

TIME

LOCATION

ENVIRONMENT

☐ FOREST	☐ GRASSLAND
☐ DESERT	☐ TUNDRA
☐ FRESHWATER	☐ MARINE

TYPE

SHAPE

WEIGHT

COLORS

TEXTURE

LUSTER

SKETCH / SAMPLE

LENGTH	WIDTH	DEPTH

EQUIPMENT

-
-
-

SETTINGS

EXTENDED DESCRIPTION

📅 DATE	
🕐 TIME	
📍 LOCATION	

ENVIRONMENT

☐ FOREST	☐ GRASSLAND
☐ DESERT	☐ TUNDRA
☐ FRESHWATER	☐ MARINE

🔺 TYPE	
🔻 SHAPE	
⚖️ WEIGHT	

⚛️ COLORS
▦ TEXTURE
✦ LUSTER

SKETCH / SAMPLE

LENGTH	WIDTH	DEPTH

EQUIPMENT

- •
- •
- •

⇄ SETTINGS

EXTENDED DESCRIPTION

📅 DATE

🕐 TIME

📍 LOCATION

ENVIRONMENT

☐ FOREST	☐ GRASSLAND
☐ DESERT	☐ TUNDRA
☐ FRESHWATER	☐ MARINE

🔻 TYPE

🔻 SHAPE

⚖️ WEIGHT

⚛️ COLORS

🗂️ TEXTURE

✨ LUSTER

SKETCH / SAMPLE

LENGTH	WIDTH	DEPTH

EQUIPMENT

-
-
-

🎚️ SETTINGS

EXTENDED DESCRIPTION

DATE

TIME

LOCATION

ENVIRONMENT

☐ FOREST	☐ GRASSLAND
☐ DESERT	☐ TUNDRA
☐ FRESHWATER	☐ MARINE

TYPE

SHAPE

WEIGHT

COLORS

TEXTURE

LUSTER

SKETCH / SAMPLE

LENGTH	WIDTH	DEPTH

EQUIPMENT

-
-
-

SETTINGS

EXTENDED DESCRIPTION

DATE

TIME

LOCATION

ENVIRONMENT

- [ ] FOREST
- [ ] GRASSLAND
- [ ] DESERT
- [ ] TUNDRA
- [ ] FRESHWATER
- [ ] MARINE

TYPE

SHAPE

WEIGHT

COLORS

TEXTURE

LUSTER

SKETCH / SAMPLE

LENGTH	WIDTH	DEPTH

EQUIPMENT

- .
- .
- .

SETTINGS

EXTENDED DESCRIPTION

DATE

TIME

LOCATION

ENVIRONMENT

☐ FOREST	☐ GRASSLAND
☐ DESERT	☐ TUNDRA
☐ FRESHWATER	☐ MARINE

TYPE

SHAPE

WEIGHT

COLORS

TEXTURE

LUSTER

SKETCH / SAMPLE

LENGTH	WIDTH	DEPTH

EQUIPMENT

-
-
-

SETTINGS

EXTENDED DESCRIPTION

📅 **DATE**	**SKETCH / SAMPLE**
🕐 **TIME**	
📍 **LOCATION**	

ENVIRONMENT

☐ FOREST	☐ GRASSLAND
☐ DESERT	☐ TUNDRA
☐ FRESHWATER	☐ MARINE

◭ **TYPE**
▽ **SHAPE**
⚖ **WEIGHT**

LENGTH	WIDTH	DEPTH

⊛ **COLORS**

▨ **TEXTURE**

✦ **LUSTER**

EQUIPMENT

-
-
-

⚊ SETTINGS

EXTENDED DESCRIPTION

📅 DATE	SKETCH / SAMPLE
🕐 TIME	
📍 LOCATION	

ENVIRONMENT

☐ FOREST	☐ GRASSLAND
☐ DESERT	☐ TUNDRA
☐ FRESHWATER	☐ MARINE

🔷 TYPE

🔻 SHAPE

⚖️ WEIGHT

LENGTH	WIDTH	DEPTH

⚛️ COLORS

🏁 TEXTURE

✨ LUSTER

EQUIPMENT

-
-
-

🎚️ SETTINGS

EXTENDED DESCRIPTION

DATE

TIME

LOCATION

ENVIRONMENT

☐ FOREST	☐ GRASSLAND
☐ DESERT	☐ TUNDRA
☐ FRESHWATER	☐ MARINE

TYPE

SHAPE

WEIGHT

COLORS

TEXTURE

LUSTER

SKETCH / SAMPLE

LENGTH	WIDTH	DEPTH

EQUIPMENT

-
-
-

SETTINGS

EXTENDED DESCRIPTION

DATE

TIME

LOCATION

ENVIRONMENT

☐ FOREST	☐ GRASSLAND
☐ DESERT	☐ TUNDRA
☐ FRESHWATER	☐ MARINE

TYPE

SHAPE

WEIGHT

COLORS

TEXTURE

LUSTER

SKETCH / SAMPLE

LENGTH	WIDTH	DEPTH

EQUIPMENT

-
-
-

SETTINGS

EXTENDED DESCRIPTION

DATE
🕐 TIME
📍 LOCATION

SKETCH / SAMPLE

LENGTH	WIDTH	DEPTH

ENVIRONMENT

☐ FOREST	☐ GRASSLAND
☐ DESERT	☐ TUNDRA
☐ FRESHWATER	☐ MARINE

🔺 TYPE
🔻 SHAPE
⚖️ WEIGHT

🎨 COLORS
🖌️ TEXTURE
✨ LUSTER

EQUIPMENT

-
-
-

🎚️ SETTINGS

EXTENDED DESCRIPTION

DATE

TIME

LOCATION

ENVIRONMENT

☐ FOREST	☐ GRASSLAND
☐ DESERT	☐ TUNDRA
☐ FRESHWATER	☐ MARINE

TYPE

SHAPE

WEIGHT

COLORS

TEXTURE

LUSTER

SKETCH / SAMPLE

LENGTH	WIDTH	DEPTH

EQUIPMENT

-
-
-

SETTINGS

EXTENDED DESCRIPTION

DATE

TIME

LOCATION

ENVIRONMENT

- ☐ FOREST
- ☐ GRASSLAND
- ☐ DESERT
- ☐ TUNDRA
- ☐ FRESHWATER
- ☐ MARINE

TYPE

SHAPE

WEIGHT

COLORS

TEXTURE

LUSTER

SKETCH / SAMPLE

LENGTH	WIDTH	DEPTH

EQUIPMENT

- .
- .
- .

SETTINGS

EXTENDED DESCRIPTION

DATE

TIME

LOCATION

ENVIRONMENT

☐ FOREST	☐ GRASSLAND
☐ DESERT	☐ TUNDRA
☐ FRESHWATER	☐ MARINE

TYPE

SHAPE

WEIGHT

COLORS

TEXTURE

LUSTER

SKETCH / SAMPLE

LENGTH	WIDTH	DEPTH

EQUIPMENT

-
-
-

SETTINGS

EXTENDED DESCRIPTION

📅 DATE	
🕐 TIME	
📍 LOCATION	

ENVIRONMENT

☐ FOREST	☐ GRASSLAND
☐ DESERT	☐ TUNDRA
☐ FRESHWATER	☐ MARINE

🔷 TYPE	
🔻 SHAPE	
⚖️ WEIGHT	

🎨 COLORS
🧵 TEXTURE
✨ LUSTER

SKETCH / SAMPLE

LENGTH	WIDTH	DEPTH

EQUIPMENT

-
-
-

🎚️ SETTINGS

EXTENDED DESCRIPTION

DATE

TIME

LOCATION

SKETCH / SAMPLE

LENGTH	WIDTH	DEPTH

ENVIRONMENT

FOREST	GRASSLAND
DESERT	TUNDRA
FRESHWATER	MARINE

TYPE

SHAPE

WEIGHT

COLORS

TEXTURE

LUSTER

EQUIPMENT

-
-
-

SETTINGS

EXTENDED DESCRIPTION

DATE

TIME

LOCATION

ENVIRONMENT

☐ FOREST	☐ GRASSLAND
☐ DESERT	☐ TUNDRA
☐ FRESHWATER	☐ MARINE

TYPE

SHAPE

WEIGHT

COLORS

TEXTURE

LUSTER

SKETCH / SAMPLE

LENGTH	WIDTH	DEPTH

EQUIPMENT

-
-
-

SETTINGS

EXTENDED DESCRIPTION

📅 DATE	
🕐 TIME	
📍 LOCATION	

SKETCH / SAMPLE

ENVIRONMENT

☐ FOREST	☐ GRASSLAND
☐ DESERT	☐ TUNDRA
☐ FRESHWATER	☐ MARINE

◭ TYPE	
▽ SHAPE	
⚖ WEIGHT	

LENGTH	WIDTH	DEPTH

⊛ COLORS	

▨ TEXTURE	

✦ LUSTER	

EQUIPMENT

-
-
-

SETTINGS

EXTENDED DESCRIPTION

DATE

TIME

LOCATION

SKETCH / SAMPLE

LENGTH	WIDTH	DEPTH

ENVIRONMENT

☐ FOREST	☐ GRASSLAND
☐ DESERT	☐ TUNDRA
☐ FRESHWATER	☐ MARINE

TYPE

SHAPE

WEIGHT

COLORS

TEXTURE

LUSTER

EQUIPMENT

- .
- .
- .

SETTINGS

EXTENDED DESCRIPTION

DATE

TIME

LOCATION

ENVIRONMENT

☐ FOREST	☐ GRASSLAND
☐ DESERT	☐ TUNDRA
☐ FRESHWATER	☐ MARINE

TYPE

SHAPE

WEIGHT

COLORS

TEXTURE

LUSTER

SKETCH / SAMPLE

LENGTH	WIDTH	DEPTH

EQUIPMENT

-
-
-

SETTINGS

EXTENDED DESCRIPTION

DATE

TIME

LOCATION

ENVIRONMENT

- [ ] FOREST
- [ ] GRASSLAND
- [ ] DESERT
- [ ] TUNDRA
- [ ] FRESHWATER
- [ ] MARINE

TYPE

SHAPE

WEIGHT

COLORS

TEXTURE

LUSTER

SKETCH / SAMPLE

LENGTH	WIDTH	DEPTH

EQUIPMENT

- .
- .
- .

SETTINGS

EXTENDED DESCRIPTION

DATE

TIME

LOCATION

ENVIRONMENT

☐ FOREST	☐ GRASSLAND
☐ DESERT	☐ TUNDRA
☐ FRESHWATER	☐ MARINE

TYPE

SHAPE

WEIGHT

COLORS

TEXTURE

LUSTER

SKETCH / SAMPLE

LENGTH	WIDTH	DEPTH

EQUIPMENT

-
-
-

SETTINGS

EXTENDED DESCRIPTION

DATE

TIME

LOCATION

ENVIRONMENT

☐ FOREST	☐ GRASSLAND
☐ DESERT	☐ TUNDRA
☐ FRESHWATER	☐ MARINE

TYPE

SHAPE

WEIGHT

COLORS

TEXTURE

LUSTER

SKETCH / SAMPLE

LENGTH	WIDTH	DEPTH

EQUIPMENT

-
-
-

SETTINGS

EXTENDED DESCRIPTION

DATE

TIME

LOCATION

ENVIRONMENT

☐ FOREST	☐ GRASSLAND
☐ DESERT	☐ TUNDRA
☐ FRESHWATER	☐ MARINE

TYPE

SHAPE

WEIGHT

COLORS

TEXTURE

LUSTER

SKETCH / SAMPLE

LENGTH	WIDTH	DEPTH

EQUIPMENT

- ·
- ·
- ·

SETTINGS

EXTENDED DESCRIPTION

DATE

TIME

LOCATION

ENVIRONMENT

☐ FOREST	☐ GRASSLAND
☐ DESERT	☐ TUNDRA
☐ FRESHWATER	☐ MARINE

TYPE

SHAPE

WEIGHT

COLORS

TEXTURE

LUSTER

SKETCH / SAMPLE

LENGTH	WIDTH	DEPTH

EQUIPMENT

-
-
-

SETTINGS

EXTENDED DESCRIPTION

DATE

TIME

LOCATION

ENVIRONMENT

☐ FOREST	☐ GRASSLAND
☐ DESERT	☐ TUNDRA
☐ FRESHWATER	☐ MARINE

TYPE

SHAPE

WEIGHT

COLORS

TEXTURE

LUSTER

SKETCH / SAMPLE

LENGTH	WIDTH	DEPTH

EQUIPMENT

-
-
-

SETTINGS

EXTENDED DESCRIPTION

DATE

TIME

LOCATION

ENVIRONMENT

☐ FOREST	☐ GRASSLAND
☐ DESERT	☐ TUNDRA
☐ FRESHWATER	☐ MARINE

TYPE

SHAPE

WEIGHT

COLORS

TEXTURE

LUSTER

SKETCH / SAMPLE

LENGTH	WIDTH	DEPTH

EQUIPMENT

-
-
-

SETTINGS

EXTENDED DESCRIPTION

DATE

TIME

LOCATION

ENVIRONMENT

☐ FOREST	☐ GRASSLAND
☐ DESERT	☐ TUNDRA
☐ FRESHWATER	☐ MARINE

TYPE

SHAPE

WEIGHT

COLORS

TEXTURE

LUSTER

SKETCH / SAMPLE

LENGTH	WIDTH	DEPTH

EQUIPMENT

-
-
-

SETTINGS

EXTENDED DESCRIPTION

DATE

TIME

LOCATION

ENVIRONMENT

☐ FOREST	☐ GRASSLAND
☐ DESERT	☐ TUNDRA
☐ FRESHWATER	☐ MARINE

TYPE

SHAPE

WEIGHT

COLORS

TEXTURE

LUSTER

SKETCH / SAMPLE

LENGTH	WIDTH	DEPTH

EQUIPMENT

-
-
-

SETTINGS

EXTENDED DESCRIPTION

DATE

TIME

LOCATION

ENVIRONMENT

☐ FOREST	☐ GRASSLAND
☐ DESERT	☐ TUNDRA
☐ FRESHWATER	☐ MARINE

TYPE

SHAPE

WEIGHT

COLORS

TEXTURE

LUSTER

SKETCH / SAMPLE

LENGTH	WIDTH	DEPTH

EQUIPMENT

-
-
-

SETTINGS

EXTENDED DESCRIPTION

📅 DATE	
⏱ TIME	
📍 LOCATION	

ENVIRONMENT

☐ FOREST	☐ GRASSLAND
☐ DESERT	☐ TUNDRA
☐ FRESHWATER	☐ MARINE

🔺 TYPE	
▽ SHAPE	
⚖ WEIGHT	

SKETCH / SAMPLE

LENGTH	WIDTH	DEPTH

⊕ COLORS	

▨ TEXTURE

✦ LUSTER

EQUIPMENT

-
-
-

⚙ SETTINGS

EXTENDED DESCRIPTION

DATE

TIME

LOCATION

ENVIRONMENT

☐ FOREST	☐ GRASSLAND
☐ DESERT	☐ TUNDRA
☐ FRESHWATER	☐ MARINE

TYPE

SHAPE

WEIGHT

COLORS

TEXTURE

LUSTER

SKETCH / SAMPLE

LENGTH	WIDTH	DEPTH

EQUIPMENT

-
-
-

SETTINGS

EXTENDED DESCRIPTION

DATE	
TIME	
LOCATION	

ENVIRONMENT

☐	FOREST	☐	GRASSLAND
☐	DESERT	☐	TUNDRA
☐	FRESHWATER	☐	MARINE

TYPE	
SHAPE	
WEIGHT	

COLORS
TEXTURE
LUSTER

SKETCH / SAMPLE

LENGTH	WIDTH	DEPTH

EQUIPMENT

-
-
-

SETTINGS

EXTENDED DESCRIPTION

DATE

TIME

LOCATION

ENVIRONMENT

☐ FOREST	☐ GRASSLAND
☐ DESERT	☐ TUNDRA
☐ FRESHWATER	☐ MARINE

TYPE

SHAPE

WEIGHT

COLORS

TEXTURE

LUSTER

SKETCH / SAMPLE

LENGTH	WIDTH	DEPTH

EQUIPMENT

- .
- .
- .

SETTINGS

EXTENDED DESCRIPTION

📅 DATE		SKETCH / SAMPLE

DATE

TIME

LOCATION

ENVIRONMENT

☐ FOREST	☐ GRASSLAND
☐ DESERT	☐ TUNDRA
☐ FRESHWATER	☐ MARINE

TYPE

SHAPE

WEIGHT

COLORS

TEXTURE

LUSTER

SKETCH / SAMPLE

LENGTH	WIDTH	DEPTH

EQUIPMENT

-
-
-

SETTINGS

EXTENDED DESCRIPTION

DATE

TIME

LOCATION

ENVIRONMENT

☐ FOREST	☐ GRASSLAND
☐ DESERT	☐ TUNDRA
☐ FRESHWATER	☐ MARINE

TYPE

SHAPE

WEIGHT

COLORS

TEXTURE

LUSTER

SKETCH / SAMPLE

LENGTH	WIDTH	DEPTH

EQUIPMENT

-
-
-

SETTINGS

EXTENDED DESCRIPTION

DATE

TIME

LOCATION

ENVIRONMENT

☐ FOREST	☐ GRASSLAND
☐ DESERT	☐ TUNDRA
☐ FRESHWATER	☐ MARINE

TYPE

SHAPE

WEIGHT

COLORS

TEXTURE

LUSTER

SKETCH / SAMPLE

LENGTH	WIDTH	DEPTH

EQUIPMENT

-
-
-

SETTINGS

EXTENDED DESCRIPTION

DATE

TIME

LOCATION

ENVIRONMENT

☐ FOREST	☐ GRASSLAND
☐ DESERT	☐ TUNDRA
☐ FRESHWATER	☐ MARINE

TYPE

SHAPE

WEIGHT

COLORS

TEXTURE

LUSTER

SKETCH / SAMPLE

LENGTH	WIDTH	DEPTH

EQUIPMENT

-
-
-

⎯ SETTINGS

EXTENDED DESCRIPTION

DATE

TIME

LOCATION

ENVIRONMENT

☐ FOREST	☐ GRASSLAND
☐ DESERT	☐ TUNDRA
☐ FRESHWATER	☐ MARINE

TYPE

SHAPE

WEIGHT

COLORS

TEXTURE

LUSTER

SKETCH / SAMPLE

LENGTH	WIDTH	DEPTH

EQUIPMENT

- .
- .
- .

SETTINGS

EXTENDED DESCRIPTION

DATE

TIME

LOCATION

ENVIRONMENT

☐ FOREST	☐ GRASSLAND
☐ DESERT	☐ TUNDRA
☐ FRESHWATER	☐ MARINE

TYPE

SHAPE

WEIGHT

COLORS

TEXTURE

LUSTER

SKETCH / SAMPLE

LENGTH	WIDTH	DEPTH

EQUIPMENT

-
-
-

SETTINGS

EXTENDED DESCRIPTION

DATE

TIME

LOCATION

ENVIRONMENT

☐ FOREST	☐ GRASSLAND
☐ DESERT	☐ TUNDRA
☐ FRESHWATER	☐ MARINE

TYPE

SHAPE

WEIGHT

COLORS

TEXTURE

LUSTER

SKETCH / SAMPLE

LENGTH	WIDTH	DEPTH

EQUIPMENT

-
-
-

⚊ SETTINGS

EXTENDED DESCRIPTION

DATE

TIME

LOCATION

ENVIRONMENT

☐ FOREST	☐ GRASSLAND
☐ DESERT	☐ TUNDRA
☐ FRESHWATER	☐ MARINE

TYPE

SHAPE

WEIGHT

COLORS

TEXTURE

LUSTER

SKETCH / SAMPLE

LENGTH	WIDTH	DEPTH

EQUIPMENT

·

·

·

SETTINGS

EXTENDED DESCRIPTION

📅 **DATE**
🕐 **TIME**
📍 **LOCATION**

SKETCH / SAMPLE

LENGTH	WIDTH	DEPTH

ENVIRONMENT

☐ FOREST	☐ GRASSLAND
☐ DESERT	☐ TUNDRA
☐ FRESHWATER	☐ MARINE

🔺 **TYPE**
🔻 **SHAPE**
⚖️ **WEIGHT**

⚛️ **COLORS**
🌫️ **TEXTURE**
✨ **LUSTER**

EQUIPMENT

-
-
-

🎚️ SETTINGS

EXTENDED DESCRIPTION

DATE

TIME

LOCATION

ENVIRONMENT

☐ FOREST	☐ GRASSLAND
☐ DESERT	☐ TUNDRA
☐ FRESHWATER	☐ MARINE

TYPE

SHAPE

WEIGHT

COLORS

TEXTURE

LUSTER

SKETCH / SAMPLE

LENGTH	WIDTH	DEPTH

EQUIPMENT

-
-
-

SETTINGS

EXTENDED DESCRIPTION

DATE

TIME

LOCATION

ENVIRONMENT

☐ FOREST	☐ GRASSLAND
☐ DESERT	☐ TUNDRA
☐ FRESHWATER	☐ MARINE

TYPE

SHAPE

WEIGHT

COLORS

TEXTURE

LUSTER

SKETCH / SAMPLE

LENGTH	WIDTH	DEPTH

EQUIPMENT

-
-
-

SETTINGS

EXTENDED DESCRIPTION

DATE

TIME

LOCATION

ENVIRONMENT

☐ FOREST	☐ GRASSLAND
☐ DESERT	☐ TUNDRA
☐ FRESHWATER	☐ MARINE

TYPE

SHAPE

WEIGHT

COLORS

TEXTURE

LUSTER

SKETCH / SAMPLE

LENGTH	WIDTH	DEPTH

EQUIPMENT

-
-
-

SETTINGS

EXTENDED DESCRIPTION

DATE

TIME

LOCATION

ENVIRONMENT

☐ FOREST	☐ GRASSLAND
☐ DESERT	☐ TUNDRA
☐ FRESHWATER	☐ MARINE

TYPE

SHAPE

WEIGHT

COLORS

TEXTURE

LUSTER

SKETCH / SAMPLE

LENGTH	WIDTH	DEPTH

EQUIPMENT

-
-
-

SETTINGS

EXTENDED DESCRIPTION

DATE

TIME

LOCATION

ENVIRONMENT

☐ FOREST	☐ GRASSLAND
☐ DESERT	☐ TUNDRA
☐ FRESHWATER	☐ MARINE

TYPE

SHAPE

WEIGHT

COLORS

TEXTURE

LUSTER

SKETCH / SAMPLE

LENGTH	WIDTH	DEPTH

EQUIPMENT

-
-
-

SETTINGS

EXTENDED DESCRIPTION

DATE		SKETCH / SAMPLE

DATE

TIME

LOCATION

ENVIRONMENT

☐ FOREST	☐ GRASSLAND
☐ DESERT	☐ TUNDRA
☐ FRESHWATER	☐ MARINE

TYPE

SHAPE

WEIGHT

SKETCH / SAMPLE

LENGTH	WIDTH	DEPTH

COLORS

TEXTURE

LUSTER

EQUIPMENT

-
-
-

SETTINGS

EXTENDED DESCRIPTION

DATE

TIME

LOCATION

ENVIRONMENT

☐ FOREST	☐ GRASSLAND
☐ DESERT	☐ TUNDRA
☐ FRESHWATER	☐ MARINE

TYPE

SHAPE

WEIGHT

COLORS

TEXTURE

LUSTER

SKETCH / SAMPLE

LENGTH	WIDTH	DEPTH

EQUIPMENT

-
-
-

SETTINGS

EXTENDED DESCRIPTION

DATE

TIME

LOCATION

ENVIRONMENT

☐ FOREST	☐ GRASSLAND
☐ DESERT	☐ TUNDRA
☐ FRESHWATER	☐ MARINE

TYPE

SHAPE

WEIGHT

COLORS

TEXTURE

LUSTER

SKETCH / SAMPLE

LENGTH	WIDTH	DEPTH

EQUIPMENT

-
-
-

SETTINGS

EXTENDED DESCRIPTION

DATE

TIME

LOCATION

ENVIRONMENT

☐ FOREST	☐ GRASSLAND
☐ DESERT	☐ TUNDRA
☐ FRESHWATER	☐ MARINE

TYPE

SHAPE

WEIGHT

COLORS

TEXTURE

LUSTER

SKETCH / SAMPLE

LENGTH	WIDTH	DEPTH

EQUIPMENT

-
-
-

SETTINGS

EXTENDED DESCRIPTION

DATE

TIME

LOCATION

ENVIRONMENT

☐ FOREST		☐ GRASSLAND
☐ DESERT		☐ TUNDRA
☐ FRESHWATER		☐ MARINE

TYPE

SHAPE

WEIGHT

COLORS

TEXTURE

LUSTER

SKETCH / SAMPLE

LENGTH	WIDTH	DEPTH

EQUIPMENT

-
-
-

SETTINGS

EXTENDED DESCRIPTION

DATE

TIME

LOCATION

ENVIRONMENT

☐ FOREST	☐ GRASSLAND
☐ DESERT	☐ TUNDRA
☐ FRESHWATER	☐ MARINE

TYPE

SHAPE

WEIGHT

COLORS

TEXTURE

LUSTER

SKETCH / SAMPLE

LENGTH	WIDTH	DEPTH

EQUIPMENT

-
-
-

SETTINGS

EXTENDED DESCRIPTION

DATE

TIME

LOCATION

ENVIRONMENT

☐ FOREST	☐ GRASSLAND
☐ DESERT	☐ TUNDRA
☐ FRESHWATER	☐ MARINE

TYPE

SHAPE

WEIGHT

COLORS

TEXTURE

LUSTER

SKETCH / SAMPLE

LENGTH	WIDTH	DEPTH

EQUIPMENT

-
-
-

SETTINGS

EXTENDED DESCRIPTION

DATE

TIME

LOCATION

ENVIRONMENT

☐ FOREST	☐ GRASSLAND
☐ DESERT	☐ TUNDRA
☐ FRESHWATER	☐ MARINE

TYPE

SHAPE

WEIGHT

COLORS

TEXTURE

LUSTER

SKETCH / SAMPLE

LENGTH	WIDTH	DEPTH

EQUIPMENT

-
-
-

SETTINGS

EXTENDED DESCRIPTION

DATE

TIME

LOCATION

ENVIRONMENT

☐ FOREST	☐ GRASSLAND
☐ DESERT	☐ TUNDRA
☐ FRESHWATER	☐ MARINE

TYPE

SHAPE

WEIGHT

COLORS

TEXTURE

LUSTER

SKETCH / SAMPLE

LENGTH	WIDTH	DEPTH

EQUIPMENT

-
-
-

SETTINGS

EXTENDED DESCRIPTION

DATE

TIME

LOCATION

ENVIRONMENT

☐ FOREST	☐ GRASSLAND
☐ DESERT	☐ TUNDRA
☐ FRESHWATER	☐ MARINE

TYPE

SHAPE

WEIGHT

COLORS

TEXTURE

LUSTER

SKETCH / SAMPLE

LENGTH	WIDTH	DEPTH

EQUIPMENT

- .
- .
- .

SETTINGS

EXTENDED DESCRIPTION

DATE

TIME

LOCATION

ENVIRONMENT

☐ FOREST	☐ GRASSLAND
☐ DESERT	☐ TUNDRA
☐ FRESHWATER	☐ MARINE

TYPE

SHAPE

WEIGHT

COLORS

TEXTURE

LUSTER

SKETCH / SAMPLE

LENGTH	WIDTH	DEPTH

EQUIPMENT

-
-
-

SETTINGS

EXTENDED DESCRIPTION

DATE

TIME

LOCATION

ENVIRONMENT

☐ FOREST	☐ GRASSLAND
☐ DESERT	☐ TUNDRA
☐ FRESHWATER	☐ MARINE

TYPE

SHAPE

WEIGHT

COLORS

TEXTURE

LUSTER

SKETCH / SAMPLE

LENGTH	WIDTH	DEPTH

EQUIPMENT

-
-
-

SETTINGS

EXTENDED DESCRIPTION

DATE

TIME

LOCATION

SKETCH / SAMPLE

ENVIRONMENT

☐ FOREST	☐ GRASSLAND
☐ DESERT	☐ TUNDRA
☐ FRESHWATER	☐ MARINE

TYPE

SHAPE

WEIGHT

LENGTH	WIDTH	DEPTH

COLORS

TEXTURE

LUSTER

EQUIPMENT

-
-
-

SETTINGS

EXTENDED DESCRIPTION

DATE

TIME

LOCATION

ENVIRONMENT

☐ FOREST	☐ GRASSLAND
☐ DESERT	☐ TUNDRA
☐ FRESHWATER	☐ MARINE

TYPE

SHAPE

WEIGHT

COLORS

TEXTURE

LUSTER

SKETCH / SAMPLE

LENGTH	WIDTH	DEPTH

EQUIPMENT

- .
- .
- .

SETTINGS

EXTENDED DESCRIPTION

DATE

TIME

LOCATION

ENVIRONMENT

- [ ] FOREST
- [ ] GRASSLAND
- [ ] DESERT
- [ ] TUNDRA
- [ ] FRESHWATER
- [ ] MARINE

TYPE

SHAPE

WEIGHT

COLORS

TEXTURE

LUSTER

SKETCH / SAMPLE

LENGTH	WIDTH	DEPTH

EQUIPMENT

- .
- .
- .

SETTINGS

EXTENDED DESCRIPTION

DATE

TIME

LOCATION

ENVIRONMENT

- [ ] FOREST
- [ ] GRASSLAND
- [ ] DESERT
- [ ] TUNDRA
- [ ] FRESHWATER
- [ ] MARINE

TYPE

SHAPE

WEIGHT

COLORS

TEXTURE

LUSTER

SKETCH / SAMPLE

LENGTH	WIDTH	DEPTH

EQUIPMENT

- •
- •
- •

SETTINGS

EXTENDED DESCRIPTION

DATE

TIME

LOCATION

ENVIRONMENT

☐ FOREST	☐ GRASSLAND
☐ DESERT	☐ TUNDRA
☐ FRESHWATER	☐ MARINE

TYPE

SHAPE

WEIGHT

COLORS

TEXTURE

LUSTER

SKETCH / SAMPLE

LENGTH	WIDTH	DEPTH

EQUIPMENT

·

·

·

SETTINGS

EXTENDED DESCRIPTION

DATE

TIME

LOCATION

ENVIRONMENT

☐ FOREST	☐ GRASSLAND
☐ DESERT	☐ TUNDRA
☐ FRESHWATER	☐ MARINE

TYPE

SHAPE

WEIGHT

COLORS

TEXTURE

LUSTER

SKETCH / SAMPLE

LENGTH	WIDTH	DEPTH

EQUIPMENT

-
-
-

SETTINGS

EXTENDED DESCRIPTION

DATE

TIME

LOCATION

ENVIRONMENT

☐ FOREST	☐ GRASSLAND
☐ DESERT	☐ TUNDRA
☐ FRESHWATER	☐ MARINE

TYPE

SHAPE

WEIGHT

COLORS

TEXTURE

LUSTER

SKETCH / SAMPLE

LENGTH	WIDTH	DEPTH

EQUIPMENT

-
-
-

SETTINGS

EXTENDED DESCRIPTION

DATE

TIME

LOCATION

ENVIRONMENT

☐ FOREST	☐ GRASSLAND
☐ DESERT	☐ TUNDRA
☐ FRESHWATER	☐ MARINE

TYPE

SHAPE

WEIGHT

COLORS

TEXTURE

LUSTER

SKETCH / SAMPLE

LENGTH	WIDTH	DEPTH

EQUIPMENT

-
-
-

SETTINGS

EXTENDED DESCRIPTION

DATE

TIME

LOCATION

ENVIRONMENT

☐ FOREST		☐ GRASSLAND	
☐ DESERT		☐ TUNDRA	
☐ FRESHWATER		☐ MARINE	

TYPE

SHAPE

WEIGHT

COLORS

TEXTURE

LUSTER

SKETCH / SAMPLE

LENGTH	WIDTH	DEPTH

EQUIPMENT

-
-
-

SETTINGS

EXTENDED DESCRIPTION

DATE

TIME

LOCATION

ENVIRONMENT

☐ FOREST	☐ GRASSLAND
☐ DESERT	☐ TUNDRA
☐ FRESHWATER	☐ MARINE

TYPE

SHAPE

WEIGHT

COLORS

TEXTURE

LUSTER

SKETCH / SAMPLE

LENGTH	WIDTH	DEPTH

EQUIPMENT

-
-
-

SETTINGS

EXTENDED DESCRIPTION

DATE

TIME

LOCATION

ENVIRONMENT

☐ FOREST	☐ GRASSLAND
☐ DESERT	☐ TUNDRA
☐ FRESHWATER	☐ MARINE

TYPE

SHAPE

WEIGHT

COLORS

TEXTURE

LUSTER

SKETCH / SAMPLE

LENGTH	WIDTH	DEPTH

EQUIPMENT

-
-
-

SETTINGS

EXTENDED DESCRIPTION

DATE

TIME

LOCATION

ENVIRONMENT

☐ FOREST	☐ GRASSLAND
☐ DESERT	☐ TUNDRA
☐ FRESHWATER	☐ MARINE

TYPE

SHAPE

WEIGHT

COLORS

TEXTURE

LUSTER

SKETCH / SAMPLE

LENGTH	WIDTH	DEPTH

EQUIPMENT

-
-
-

SETTINGS

EXTENDED DESCRIPTION

DATE	SKETCH / SAMPLE
TIME	
LOCATION	

ENVIRONMENT

☐ FOREST	☐ GRASSLAND
☐ DESERT	☐ TUNDRA
☐ FRESHWATER	☐ MARINE

TYPE

SHAPE

WEIGHT

LENGTH	WIDTH	DEPTH

COLORS

TEXTURE

LUSTER

EQUIPMENT

-
-
-

SETTINGS

EXTENDED DESCRIPTION

DATE

TIME

LOCATION

ENVIRONMENT

☐ FOREST	☐ GRASSLAND
☐ DESERT	☐ TUNDRA
☐ FRESHWATER	☐ MARINE

TYPE

SHAPE

WEIGHT

COLORS

TEXTURE

LUSTER

SKETCH / SAMPLE

LENGTH	WIDTH	DEPTH

EQUIPMENT

-
-
-

SETTINGS

EXTENDED DESCRIPTION

DATE

TIME

LOCATION

ENVIRONMENT

☐ FOREST	☐ GRASSLAND
☐ DESERT	☐ TUNDRA
☐ FRESHWATER	☐ MARINE

TYPE

SHAPE

WEIGHT

COLORS

TEXTURE

LUSTER

SKETCH / SAMPLE

LENGTH	WIDTH	DEPTH

EQUIPMENT

-
-
-

SETTINGS

EXTENDED DESCRIPTION

📅 **DATE**
🕐 **TIME**
📍 **LOCATION**

ENVIRONMENT

☐ FOREST	☐ GRASSLAND
☐ DESERT	☐ TUNDRA
☐ FRESHWATER	☐ MARINE

🔺 **TYPE**
▽ **SHAPE**
⚖ **WEIGHT**

SKETCH / SAMPLE

LENGTH	WIDTH	DEPTH

⊛ **COLORS**
🗥 **TEXTURE**
✦ **LUSTER**

EQUIPMENT

- .
- .
- .

⇌ SETTINGS

EXTENDED DESCRIPTION

DATE

TIME

LOCATION

ENVIRONMENT

☐ FOREST	☐ GRASSLAND
☐ DESERT	☐ TUNDRA
☐ FRESHWATER	☐ MARINE

TYPE

SHAPE

WEIGHT

COLORS

TEXTURE

LUSTER

SKETCH / SAMPLE

LENGTH	WIDTH	DEPTH

EQUIPMENT

-
-
-

SETTINGS

EXTENDED DESCRIPTION

| 📅 **DATE** |
| 🕐 **TIME** |
| 📍 **LOCATION** |

ENVIRONMENT

☐ FOREST	☐ GRASSLAND
☐ DESERT	☐ TUNDRA
☐ FRESHWATER	☐ MARINE

| ⬢ **TYPE** |
| ▽ **SHAPE** |
| ⚖ **WEIGHT** |

SKETCH / SAMPLE

LENGTH	WIDTH	DEPTH

| ⊛ **COLORS** |
| |
| ⦚ **TEXTURE** |
| |
| ✦ **LUSTER** |
| |

EQUIPMENT

- ·
- ·
- ·

⚙ SETTINGS

EXTENDED DESCRIPTION

DATE

TIME

LOCATION

ENVIRONMENT

☐ FOREST	☐ GRASSLAND
☐ DESERT	☐ TUNDRA
☐ FRESHWATER	☐ MARINE

TYPE

SHAPE

WEIGHT

COLORS

TEXTURE

LUSTER

SKETCH / SAMPLE

LENGTH	WIDTH	DEPTH

EQUIPMENT

- .
- .
- .

SETTINGS

EXTENDED DESCRIPTION

Notes

Notes

Made in the USA
Middletown, DE
18 December 2023

46170512R00066